The City That Could Not Be Broken "Ypres"

Almeyda Fernandez

United States
2024

Imprint

Book Title: The City That Could Not Be Broken "Ypres"
Author: Almeyda Fernandez

Author: Almeyda Fernandez
Contact: slushydoe@gmail.com

CONTENTS

I. The Paris

From the vantage point of the balcony, the view below is nothing short of mesmerizing. The sprawling tree-tops below resemble a vast forest, their trunks concealed in a tangled web of alleyways and squares, as if viewed from the summit of a towering mountain. These trees, firmly rooted in the soil of French history, are not mere flora; they symbolize the essence of the land they thrive on. On the dusty gravel promenade that runs between the verdant garden and the bustling street, two young figures, a man and a woman, are engaged in a spirited game with rackets—one of the many second-rate ball games favored by the petite bourgeoisie of France. Their jackets and hats rest on the edge of a quaint wooden box that holds a flourishing orange tree. The pair, drenched in sweat from the heat of the early morning sun, are undoubtedly in love. Their playful interaction, seemingly frivolous and insignificant, is a contrast to the weight of the world outside their bubble. It feels almost absurd, this delicate dance of affection, at a time and place so fraught with tension. They seem unaware, or perhaps simply unbothered, by the reality of the profound crisis unfolding around them—one that threatens to consume everything they know and love.

From this same balcony, the landmarks of Paris stand in striking proximity. The Louvre stretches out before you, its sculptures ranging from the works of Jean Goujon to the masterpieces of Carpeaux; the Church of St. Clotilde, where the genius of César Franck was hidden for decades, untouched by the limelight; the Quai d'Orsay railway station, a marvel of architecture that proved a terminus could evoke the same emotions as a palace or temple; the dome of the Invalides, standing proud against the skyline;

and the majestic facades surrounding the Place de la Concorde, housing the Ministry of Marine. For anyone who understands Paris—not just as a city, but as a symbol of human achievement—the sight is deeply moving. The artistry of the Ministry of Marine, with its exquisite plinths, mouldings, and carvings, serves as a testament to the heights of national craftsmanship. To gaze upon it is to be transported to a place of profound respect and admiration.

And yet, the prevailing feeling is one of profound escape. All this beauty, all this heritage, was at one point perilously close to destruction. It was under threat from forces who understood its value even less than the young couple with their rackets, forces whose awareness was only a whisper compared to the grandeur of the civilization they sought to dismantle. These were beings whose cruelty was as savage as their ignorance was boundless. Paris stood at the edge of catastrophe, but miraculously, it survived. No city was ever in greater danger, and yet, by some stroke of fortune, it managed to avert disaster. The streets had been lined with taxi cabs carrying the Sixth Army—the last hope of salvation—rushing forward at an unimaginable pace, turning the tide of battle and, perhaps, the course of history itself.

"The population of Paris has revolted and is coming to beg for mercy from us!" the German scouts thought, mistaking the flurry of taxi cabs racing north for a sign of panic. But what they had actually witnessed was the swift movement of the Sixth Army, whose arrival would mark the turning point of the campaign. The German officer, realizing the mistake the next day, could only reflect, "A great misfortune has overtaken us." Indeed, it was far greater than he could have ever anticipated.

The terror of what could have been, coupled with the awe of what actually transpired, fills the mind with a sense of awe as you gaze upon Paris from the balcony. The city, against all odds, had escaped. The event was not just a close call—it was a moment of sheer wonder, one that is impossible to fully grasp. It is too grand, too momentous, for the mind to fully comprehend.

The streets of Paris, though still recovering, now bear a peculiar calm, as if it were a Sunday morning. The usual hum of activity has been replaced by a tranquil stillness, punctuated by the occasional rumble of returning taxi cabs. The auto-buses, once a staple of Parisian life, are nowhere to be found, having retreated behind the front lines. The underground railways, now manned by women, have become the primary mode of transport. A horse-drawn bus, seemingly resurrected from a bygone era, clatters down the grand boulevards, its driver—a stout, cheerful peasant woman—gathering fares in the ample folds of her black apron. Many of the most extravagant and unnecessary shops remain shuttered, while others sit quietly in anticipation of the return of business. Yet, the humble provision shops, the lifeblood of the working-class neighborhoods, continue to operate as usual, without fanfare or self-consciousness. The streets are filled with soldiers in a wild array of uniforms—some in pale blue, others in black—all jumbled together in a chaotic but somehow unified display. The pavements are dotted with widows and orphans, their grief profound yet unspoken. The young girls and women in mourning are numerous, their heavy black veils the only visible casualty list allowed by the French War Office.

Paris, once so full of energy and glamour, now seems a place transformed—odd, yet still unmistakably itself. Amid the growing realization of a disaster narrowly avoided, and the dawning awareness of the power the French nation now wields, the spirit of Paris stands resolute. The French have come to understand their own identity anew. They are angered, but coldly so; they are not defeated, but they are changed. To witness this transformation is nothing short of inspiring. Paris is under a spell, an enchantment that magnifies the beauty of its resilience even as the mundane details of daily life continue to unfold, oddly persistent.

In a small sixth-floor apartment, one might find a stark contrast to the grandeur of the city below. The kitchen, modest with only two gas rings for cooking, could easily be imagined beneath the roots of an orange tree in the Tuileries gardens. The apartment is neat to an almost obsessive degree, every item carefully chosen and cherished. One such item is a watercolour painting, long forgotten but now framed and displayed with pride. The apartment's sole occupant, a spinster seamstress in her thirties, earns a modest three francs a day, yet she is rich in her simplicity. Her wealth comes not from material possessions, but from the quiet discipline of living within her means. Despite her unassuming nature, she harbors a fiery temper that only two things can provoke: any mention of marriage or any attempt to alter her established routines. These are the sacred pillars of her existence. Her visit to a small town last summer, to assist her sister-in-law with running a café, was meant to be a holiday of sorts. Yet, she could not bear the thought of standing for hours, serving a crowd she barely understood. Eventually, the pull of Parisian life became irresistible, and she returned, despite the escalating war around her. The journey was grueling, taking three days and two nights, filled with refugees and wounded soldiers. Yet, she persisted. Upon returning to Paris, she was greeted by the news that the Germans had left the café untouched, though the war had certainly left its mark.

When asked about the journey, she simply states, "It was terrible. A three-hour journey turned into three days of standing, no space to move, and very little food or drink." And yet, in the end, she had made it back. The war had disrupted her life, but not her spirit. Through all of it, she remained unchanged, her habits as unwavering as ever.

And then, there is the Boulevard St. Germain—an old, grand home, a relic of another era. The drawing room, locked away for two decades, still bears the heavy, sombre furnishings of a time gone by. The matriarch, a widow of formidable will, is as active as any woman half her age. She rises at five in the morning, and no cook has ever quite satisfied her standards. Her son, a bachelor of fifty, is paralyzed and spends his days in a wheeled chair, surrounded by books, engravings, and newspapers. Their conversations often turn to investments, the war, and the uncertain future ahead. Despite the dire circumstances, the elderly widow remains resolute, never quite believing that the Germans will be defeated. "They will never be beaten," she insists, "because they are always capable of inventing something new." She continues, undeterred, to run her household with the same precision and authority she has always possessed.

In contrast to this family's tenacity is the story of a fashionable dressmaker, a beautiful woman whose life has been turned upside down by the war. Her husband, once a soldier, now holds a small administrative post, while their two young sons remain the picture of youthful Parisian elegance. Yet, despite the surface beauty of their life, the war has strained their resources. Her workshop, once bustling with seventy employees, now stands empty. The dressmaker reflects on the hardships brought on by the war, noting that the simplest things, like salt and chicory, had become impossible to obtain. Still, she remains hopeful, waiting for the return of normalcy, and though the war has left its mark, her spirit remains unbroken.

Through these stories, Paris, both as a city and as a symbol, reveals its true essence. Despite the chaos, despite the fear, it endures. And in that endurance, there is a beauty that cannot be extinguished.

In the final moments of our gathering, I found myself in the heart of Paris, in a home famous for the richness of its eclectic collection. It was a place of both old and new—bric-a-brac, porcelain, exquisite fans, and furniture interspersed with modern paintings that filled the walls. Among the artworks were frescoes by Pierre Bonnard and his contemporaries, creating an atmosphere both refined and contemporary. From a black marble balcony, the view was nothing short of breathtaking, offering a rare perspective of Paris, the very center of the city. This was a place where worlds collided: authors, musicians, painters, administrators, and casual admirers all gathered in the same space.

The hostess, ever gracious, had invited a high-ranking official from the Foreign Office, someone I had not seen in many years. While she didn't explicitly say so, it was clear her intention was to facilitate my travels to the war zone, an endeavor I had long been planning. Several of my old friends were also present, and it was astonishing to see how many had managed to avoid active service—some by necessity due to their roles in administration, others due to neutral stances, or because they were deemed too old or physically unfit for service. A few had, unfortunately, perished in the line of duty, leaving an empty space in the room.

Amid the beautiful chaos of objects that demanded admiration, conversation inevitably turned to the war. The Foreign Office official, dressed in pale alpaca and yellow boots, explained with a calm authority the meanings behind various colored books—Yellow Books, White Books, Orange Books, Blue Books. But the true, more pressing matters were left untouched. Music played, including Schumann, a German composer, which added a strange yet profound air of normalcy to the proceedings. Then literature came to the forefront. One novelist, eager to engage, asked me my opinion on a book titled The Way of All Flesh. He was surprised to learn that it was still making waves internationally, even though it had been written so long ago. He also expressed curiosity about George Gissing, a name that was new to him.

Suddenly, from the dimly lit corner of the balcony, a voice interrupted, startling me. It was a question that seemed out of place in the midst of such cultured discourse:

"Sincerely, do they hate the Germans in England? Do they truly hate them? I doubt it. I doubt it strongly."

I laughed awkwardly, as any Englishman might, taken aback by the question's bluntness. The fleeting episode, though brief, disrupted the flow of conversation and shifted our focus from literature to a more uncomfortable topic.

As the night wore on, discussions about my proposed visit to the front faltered. While the trip had been arranged, scheduling the actual departure seemed impossible. So, I opted for a visit to Meaux, a place I had long been fascinated by due to its historical and literary significance. Meaux had been burned by the Normans in the tenth century and witnessed horrific massacres in the fourteenth century—events that featured prominently in English history, particularly for the aristocracy. In the seventeenth century, it had also been the seat of the renowned Bishop Bossuet. But most recently, during the First World War, the Germans had advanced to Meaux before being stopped just short of Paris. Meaux had thus become a symbol, the nearest point to Paris reached by enemy forces.

Even a trip to Meaux required certain formalities. The journey, which would have taken half the time by car, was delayed by the slow pace of the train that meandered along the Marne. But the formalities were simple. Meaux, a town with a population of just fourteen thousand, was dominated by its cathedral, so much so that when viewed from a distance, the town seemed to consist entirely of this imposing structure.

Upon arriving, we hired a carriage driven by a solemn, elderly man who, with little enthusiasm, offered to take us to Barcy, a village that had been bombarded and burned during the war. For fifteen francs, plus a tip, he agreed to show us the battlefield. His calm, almost resigned demeanor, as he pointed out the villages along the route, added an eerie sense of melancholy to the journey. As we passed through the villages of Penchard, Poincy, and Monthyon, the driver spoke of German scouts who had briefly occupied Meaux, believing that they were facing a much larger force than they actually were.

Our driver explained how the Germans had been tricked by English headquarters in La Ferte-sous-Jouarre, who had blown up a bridge as a precaution. He then pointed out the first tomb—a simple yet poignant grave, marked by a white flag, a cross, and a small wreath. The grave of a soldier from the 66th Territorials was a symbol of the last desperate push of the Germans before their retreat.

As we continued, we crossed an expansive plain dotted with patches of forest, fields of wheat, and the occasional tombstone. The area had once been a site of bloody conflict, but now, in the calm aftermath, it had been reclaimed by nature. The earth, though still scarred by the trenches, was now covered by crops and wildflowers. The land was slowly healing, though the memory of the war lingered in the quiet graves scattered across the landscape. Some tombs were marked by white flags and crosses, while others were simply numbered, their occupants unknown.

We came upon a farmhouse that had been gutted by the Germans. The furniture was looted, and the wine casks were smashed. The sight of this abandoned home, once filled with familiar objects, now left empty and broken, was a powerful reminder of the war's destruction. The house stood as a silent testament to the lives disrupted by the conflict.

Barcy, once a key battleground, loomed ahead. The church tower, though shattered, still stood as a symbol of resilience. We passed through the village, which had been rebuilt but still showed signs of the brutal fighting. Some houses had been restored with new red roofs, while others remained in ruin. The post office, severely damaged, had yet to be fully repaired, and the church, with its broken roof and shattered windows, was a haunting sight. Inside, the pews remained largely intact, but the altar and nave were a chaotic mess of destruction.

As we left Barcy, we drove through a landscape dotted with more tombs—white crosses marking the graves of soldiers. But there were also darker crosses, black ones, signifying the graves of German soldiers. These graves, devoid of names or wreaths, served as a stark reminder of the enemy that had once occupied this land. The contrast between the white and black crosses was striking, symbolizing the deep divisions created by the war.

As we made our way back to Meaux, the fields, once battlegrounds, were now covered in crops, which seemed to ignore the tombs beneath them, growing over them as if in defiance of the war's lingering presence. The wheat and oats, ripe for harvest, were a testament to nature's resilience.

Finally, after a long day of reflection and remembrance, we returned to the ordinary, matter-of-fact railway station in Meaux. In the café, a Frenchwoman served us tea as if nothing out of the ordinary had occurred. Yet, as we returned to Paris, I knew that the experience of visiting the front, of seeing the graves and the remnants of battle, would stay with me forever. It was a powerful reminder that the front lines, though distant, had once been closer than we dared imagine.

II. French Front

We were greeted at the poste de commandment by the officers in charge, who had been expecting us. It soon became clear that this was a common occurrence. Whether it was a General, Colonel, or Commandant, at every stop, the highest-ranking officer would be present to explain the situation. And they explained everything with a clarity that only the French seem to possess—an extraordinary gift, as demonstrated in the official reports detailing the earlier phases of the war, which had been shared with the Anglo-Saxon public through Reuter.

Our small group of four was accompanied by an abundance of automobiles and chauffeurs. At no point during the day, whether we were speeding along bumpy, deteriorating roads or walking the land, did I lack a staff officer by my side. Each one gave me the impression that they existed solely to be of service to me. Every detail of our journey was carefully organized, and the entire operation ran smoothly. No pre-Lusitania American correspondent could have been more pampered by the Germans, who were desperate for his favor, than I was spoiled by the French, who had already won my goodwill without needing to try.

After the formalities of greeting, we ascended to a high terrace of a large chateau nearby. From there, a vast expanse of France spread out before us in a shimmering semicircle. In the distance, a low range of hills, irregularly dotted with trees, marked the horizon. A river snaked its way through the landscape, flowing into patches of dense woodland and small copses. Beyond that, endless vineyards stretched upward in varying slopes, creeping out of the valley nearly to our feet. Far to the left, a town with towering factory chimneys stood silently, smoke-free.

Peasant women bent low in the vineyards, while the earth seemed to be alive with cultivation, yielding abundantly. The scene was a magnificent one, set against a glorious summer afternoon. The sun hung high in the sky, casting huge purple shadows that moved slowly across the vibrant greens of the land. The air was filled with a sense of peace, majesty, and the quiet richness of the French soil.

"You see that white line on the hills over there?" one of the officers asked, unfolding a large-scale map.

I guessed it was a road.

"That's the German trenches," he explained. "They're five miles away, and their gun positions are hidden in the woods. Our own trenches are invisible from here."

It was a monumental moment—the first time I laid eyes on the German trenches. The sight brought a mix of awe and deep sorrow. My thoughts raced: All of France beyond that line, land just like the one on which I stand, inhabited by people just like those around me, is under the oppressive tyranny of invaders. As I tried to comprehend the scale, the realization hit me—these trenches spanned from Ostend to Switzerland, and the same men who had built them were engaged in similar operations as far northeast as Riga and as far southeast as the borders of Romania. In that moment, I thought, These brigands may be mad, but they are mad in a grand, terrifying way.

We had arrived at the front.

For the last twenty miles, we had driven along a heavily patrolled road, closed to civilians. Even the staff officers had to pass through sentries, whispering passwords to avoid being turned away. Civilian life in this area had been suspended, existing precariously from one meal to the next. Aeroplanes roared overhead, shattering any semblance of peace. No letter could leave a post office without a mandatory delay of three days, and telegrams were highly suspect. Gaining entry to a railway station was nearly as difficult as entering a fortress, and only those with passports or special passes could enjoy the restricted freedoms that remained. Yet, amid all this, I saw no signs of distress. No one frowned or complained. Everyone seemed to accept the necessity of these measures in service of the immense military machine. They waited, calmly and with confident smiles.

It would be inaccurate to say that civilian life had come to a halt. Beneath the layers of military control, the fundamental aspects of life went on. The land continued to yield, and the crops flourished, all the way up to the very edge of the German wire entanglements. Officers warned the peasants of the danger, but they simply responded, The land must be worked.

When the German artillery began to fire, the blue-clad women would disappear into the shelter of the woods. A half hour after the barrage ceased, they would cautiously reemerge and continue their work. One peasant, seemingly unconcerned, even set up an umbrella for shade—though it was a man.

We were undeniably at the front. But at that moment, the front seemed more abstract than real. No sounds of battle, no signs of destruction—just the faint, pale line of the German trenches, barely visible on the distant hills. A distant rumble of thunder reverberated through the air. It was the sound of gunfire. A small puff of smoke appeared in the distance. Yet, this brief disturbance did nothing to mar the serenity of the landscape. The whole scene seemed indifferent to the war that loomed just beyond it. But even in this calm, we knew we were on the cusp of something vast and dangerous.

A little further along, we were shown the aftermath of a previous artillery strike—a massive crater gouged into the earth. The sight of this sudden destruction made the war feel less abstract, more real.

"There are eighty thousand men in front of us," one of the officers said, gesturing toward the landscape.

"But where?" I asked, struggling to understand.

"Buried—in the trenches," he replied.

It seemed unbelievable.

I turned to ask, "And the others—the dead?"

"We never speak of them," came the quiet reply. "But we think of them often."

A little closer to the war zone, we visited the parc du génie—the engineers' park—where we saw hills of coils of barbed wire, far more dangerous than anything farmers used. These coils seemed designed not just to trap, but to tear apart anyone who came too close. There were also stacks of timber for shoring up mines, sacks of earth for makeshift entrenchments, and chevaux de frise—four-pointed devices designed to impale anyone unlucky enough to get caught in them. Even tarred paper was stored for use in keeping trenches dry. The quantities of supplies were staggering.

Nearby, a small group of German prisoners were performing menial labor under guard. They moved about, resigned, as though they knew the war was far from over. One officer told us that when he had mentioned the possibility of exchanging prisoners, the Germans had protested, preferring captivity over returning to the horrors of the front. The prisoners looked brutalized, a stark reminder of the dehumanizing effects of war.

Not far from this, we toured a hospital—a ambulance de première ligne—set up in a factory. This was the first stop for the wounded, who arrived directly from the dressing stations behind the front lines. A telephone call summoned an automobile, which often arrived before the stretcher-bearers. The injured could be operated on within an hour of being wounded, though many of the hospital's staff and equipment were mobile, able to relocate quickly as needed.

One hospital had once been evacuated entirely within sixty minutes, responding swiftly to an order for a sudden transfer. We toured the facility, passing through small wards, operating rooms, and storage areas, all pungent with the smell of ether. The patients were few, but the weariness on the doctor's face told the story of the immense labor that must have taken place behind those closed doors.

In the vast courtyard, we found a tent hospital, ready to move on short notice. The medical staff worked quietly within, preparing for the next crisis, while outside, a wagon with sterilizing equipment waited, ready to be deployed at a moment's notice.

Our tour continued with a visit to an aviation park, set in a vast wheatfield atop a hill. There, we saw hangars housing planes used to direct artillery fire. The planes had their own transport vehicles—sometimes they needed to be transported by road if they were damaged. The officer in charge, a young non-commissioned officer with a southern accent, demonstrated the capabilities of the planes, showing us their wireless equipment and giving us a chance to sit in the cockpit. Despite the unsuitable weather for flying, he revved the engine, producing a draft that bent the wheat behind us and blew our hats off.

Afterward, we were shown anti-aircraft guns, specially designed to bring down enemy planes. The officer gave us a detailed explanation of the guns' workings, which lasted nearly half an hour, though much of it was beyond my understanding. It was clear, however, that these guns were built to hit their targets with deadly accuracy.

Our final stop was at a seventy-five—the famous French artillery piece. We observed its operation, the precision with which it was loaded and fired, and the speed of its recoil. When we suggested testing it out, the officer immediately agreed. Within moments, the gun was ready to fire. With a sharp bang, the shell was launched, its trajectory invisible, its destination unknown. A second shell was fired for good measure, and the artillerymen stood ready, prepared for whatever came next.

We embark on another descent into the earth, venturing a few yards further when, unexpectedly, the trench splits into three directions. Confusion sets in. We are unsure which path to follow, and the officer behind us, as lost as we are, has no idea either. The officer who should be leading us is a good thirty yards ahead, and despite our calls, there is no response. We scramble out of the trench, emerging onto the surface, where a desolate wasteland stretches as far as the eye can see. There is no sign of our comrades, not even a trace of their tracks. The ground, untouched by human presence, seems to mock us. This, in itself, serves as a grim testament to the vastness and isolation of trench warfare.

After a moment of panic, an officer finally appears, guiding us to the correct path, the trench on the far right. We continue, walking in the oppressive heat, completely disoriented. Our sense of direction is lost entirely.

Eventually, we reach a portion of the road where a railway crosses. In the distance, we spot a German captive balloon, motionless against the sky. The railway, once a symbol of progress and efficiency, now stands abandoned, its signal wires hanging like limp ribbons, its tracks rusting away. The sight is haunting. It is almost incomprehensible to witness such neglect of a main line in what was once a thriving, civilized country. One begins to question whether we are witnessing the remnants of a lost civilization, its soul erased by the madness of war.

This particular stretch of railway is useless to both the Germans and the French. It lies within French territory but is too exposed to German artillery to be of any use. About ten kilometers of the tracks remain, serving as a tragic monument to the senselessness of the invasion. It is a place that evokes despair.

The journey continues, and we finally arrive at a village that lies at the tip of a French salient. The sight before us is heart-wrenching. The village has been utterly destroyed. The ruins are a grim spectacle of war. Amidst the rubble, we spot strange, disquieting remnants: a teddy bear resting on the broken steps of a staircase, a bedframe half-buried in debris, and the skeletal remains of birds in a cage that still hangs on a wall. The entire area is a hotbed of bombardment, its inhabitants caught in a relentless cycle of violence. Yet, in spite of the chaos, a few civilians refuse to leave. Seventeen in total—seven men and ten women—remain stubbornly in place. I speak with one elderly woman, who insists that there is no danger, that life must go on. A moment later, a shell explodes just a hundred yards from where we stand. It is a sobering reminder of the absurdity of her belief, and the cruel reality of the war that surrounds us.

The village church, once a place of sanctuary, is now a shadow of its former self. Its roof is gone, though two thin arches remain, seemingly defying gravity. A few sad flowers are arranged on the altar. Despite the destruction, Mass is still celebrated every Sunday, a testament to the endurance of the human spirit. We meet the village priest, a frail man wearing the Legion of Honour. In his eyes, we can see both the weight of his years and the unwavering resolve that has kept him in this forsaken place.

We continue our journey through the trenches, which now seem like a maze of subterranean passages. The heat of the sun is felt but not seen. Signs on the walls, such as "Tranchee de repli," or "Guetteur de jour et de nuit" (watcher by day and by night), point the way. We open one door, and inside, we encounter a pale man who appears almost ghostly, standing vigil in the gloom. He says nothing, but his silent presence is unsettling.

Beyond this, we catch a glimpse of an abandoned road and a sprawling network of barbed wire. Our path winds further, and we arrive at a makeshift redoubt constructed from crumbling homes and stables. The sound of rifle fire rings out in the distance, but we cannot see the source. We are shown the machine gun chamber, where the muzzle aperture is briefly uncovered, and then we are led underground to a refuge, a shelter from the inevitable bombardments.

We then make our way to the quarters of the men, where we are greeted with a resounding "Bonjour, les poilus!" from the Commandant. His bright smile and lively gestures are infectious. The soldiers salute with pride and enthusiasm, their demeanor filled with a fierce sense of devotion. One soldier in particular stands out—a man with a sharp gaze and a strong presence. His body language speaks of unwavering confidence, as if saying, "I know my worth, and I am utterly dedicated to this cause." A young officer remarks that these men possess both the wildness of a beast and the purity of an angel—a profound observation, one I can't help but admire.

The regiment, stationed in the village since autumn, has refused to be relieved, and their energy seems as fresh as if they had just arrived. The comfort of the soldiers is surprising. They have created small gardens with statues, a gymnasium for recreation, and even a theatre with a stage and costumes. This, in contrast to the chaos outside, speaks to the resilience and adaptability of these men.

Our final destination is the first-line trench, and the experience is unlike anything we've seen before. The trench, although swept clean and well-maintained, bears little resemblance to the grim, mud-filled channels we've come to associate with warfare. Instead, it resembles a long wooden gallery. Its sides, ceiling, and floor are all constructed of wood, and though the craftsmanship is rudimentary, it is functional and surprisingly neat.

We are told that no engineers have been involved in the construction, yet it is regarded as one of the most ingenious positions on the front. The trench is dimly lit, with small loop-holes providing narrow, but crucial, views of the area outside. The loop-holes are arranged in such a way that soldiers can aim their weapons through them without fully exposing themselves to enemy fire. Each loop-hole is labeled with the name of the soldier assigned to it, and between the gaps, there are photographs and postcards of loved ones—a poignant reminder of the lives they are fighting to protect.

As we peer through the loop-holes, we see the enemy's trenches in the distance, separated from us by a strip of desolate land. The proximity of the two sides is palpable. The trench warfare that defines this conflict is an inescapable reality for both the French and the Germans. The tension is suffocating, and it becomes clear that this war is not just a matter of strategy and resources, but of survival.

As we leave the trench and return to the Commandant's quarters, we are greeted with more champagne. The celebration is a welcome reprieve from the horrors of the front, and the atmosphere is one of camaraderie and respect. The Commandant, with his unshakable confidence and charm, presides over the gathering. His leadership, like that of many others in the French army, inspires admiration and loyalty.

In a final moment of levity, we are told the story of a Lieutenant who, in the midst of battle, asked the village priest if he might celebrate Mass. The priest's response was simple but profound: "If you are a priest, then you may." And so, the Lieutenant, in his uniform and amidst the destruction, celebrated Mass for his men.

As we prepare to leave, the sound of artillery fire echoes in the distance. The tension is palpable once more. We quickly move to the trench, bending low as explosions rock the earth around us. The officers instruct us to count to five before rising, a precaution against the shrapnel that follows the initial explosion. We move cautiously, keeping our heads down and our senses alert.

In this war, time and space lose all meaning. The front lines are a place of constant danger, where life and death are separated by mere inches. Yet, amidst the violence and destruction, there remains an undeniable sense of purpose, a belief that, despite everything, victory is still within reach.

III. Ruins Left

When traveling into Rheims along the Epernay road, the scene that greets you appears typical at first glance—life moves forward as usual. There are no longer the once-necessary customs checks, and the streets are filled with the bustle of daily life. Women—some young and striking—look on indifferently as your car passes by. Children run and shout in the warmth of the sun, enjoying their carefree play. The small cafes and shops keep their doors open, busy with daily transactions. The baker is hard at work, and middle-aged locals continue their quiet routines, deep in thought. Soldiers are present, but that's not unusual; soldiers are stationed in nearly every major town across France, even in peacetime. In short, the scene looks much like any of the poorer outer streets on the way to the city center.

However, in less than two minutes, everything changes. A short drive and you enter a quarter where life has completely disappeared. This area has not just been damaged—it has been obliterated. The buildings, although still standing in parts, are ruined beyond repair. They will need to be rebuilt from the ground up, starting with the cellars. This area is a wasteland, untouched by life, a testament to destruction. Large houses, small homes, and shops have all suffered equally. The facades may stand—some still intact while others lean precariously—but the interiors are nothing but a heap of debris. In some places, entire floors have vanished, leaving only exposed walls. In others, floors hang at strange angles, defying gravity. What was once a home or a place of business has now turned into an unrecognizable pile of ruin. Among the piles of rubble, fragments of intimate household items can be seen: a bathtub, part of a mirror, a piece of tapestry, a saucepan. Even a funeral wreath still hangs in its shop, a bizarre remnant of normal life. Telephone and telegraph wires hang loosely, tangled from broken poles. The clock on the Protestant church is frozen at a quarter to six.

The shells fired by the enemy seem capricious in their destruction. One shell simply makes a hole in the courtyard large enough to bury a whole German army, while another, a powerful 210 mm shell, punches through an inner wall, opening up the cellars beneath. Incredibly, ten people are sheltering there, and miraculously, none are harmed. Meanwhile, old shop signs—such as "The Good Hope" and "The Success of the Day"—remain hanging, their message now almost mocking in the face of the catastrophe.

The inhabitants of this quarter, and many others in Rheims, are gone. Some have perished, while others have fled to places like Epernay or Paris. They left everything behind—yet in a sense, they left nothing. The tragedy is so vast, so unfathomable, that it is impossible to fully grasp the scope of it. Yet, amidst the horror, there is a strange beauty in the ruin—oddly, even in the destruction of modern architecture, the ruins occasionally take on a certain form of grandeur. The image of a pale bedroom wall-paper contrasting against blackened masonry, with part of a house jutting up like a jagged column amidst the chaos, sticks in the mind. It serves as a symbol of the damage wrought by the German forces.

This destruction is not accidental—it is precisely what the Germans intended when they crossed into France. The annihilation of homes, businesses, and lives, the transformation of joy into sorrow, was the goal all along. This was the work of military planners and leaders, who devised this destruction with cold, scientific intent. The cruelty of it is obvious, but what's even more devastating is the sheer futility of it. The senselessness overwhelms the mind. This destruction, born of political greed, seems even more monstrous than if it were sparked by religious conflict. It is an abhorrent anachronism, a tragic relic of a past era that seems out of place in the modern world.

Curiously, in a nearby quarter—one that has not been completely obliterated—a man arrives home in a cab, luggage in tow. The servant-girl waits at the door, offering a brief reminder that life, in some pockets, continues. In another oddity, a property-owner who had begun building a house just before the war has resumed construction in the midst of all this chaos. And in the Esplanade Ceres, the fountain continues to flow serenely, despite the surrounding devastation, while German trenches lie just two miles away.

It is impossible for anyone with a sense of reason to look at the geography of this destruction without concluding that the Germans were specifically targeting the Cathedral. Tracing the streets that have borne the brunt of the assault, one can clearly see that the Germans were attempting to hit the Cathedral with their shelling. The majority of the damage centers around this iconic structure.

Yet, remarkably, the Cathedral stands.

Though the area surrounding it is leveled, with hotels and the Archbishop's palace in ruins, the Cathedral remains defiant amidst the devastation. The outer roof is gone, much of the masonry has crumbled, and many of the statues have been destroyed or warped into grotesque, tortured forms. But in its core and shape, the Cathedral remains a testament to endurance. The towers, though scarred, stand strong and dignified, their solemn presence unshaken. Yes, the damage is immense—the intricate carvings, the glass windows, and the decorative interiors are mostly gone—but the Cathedral's structural integrity has withstood the onslaught of German artillery. It will never be the same, but it exists—still a beacon of defiance in the face of overwhelming odds.

The Germans, perhaps in frustration, seem to use the Cathedral as a target for their fury. They fire shells at it not because it holds any strategic value, but because it represents something they despise—a symbol of French pride and civilization. The French attempted to shield it by removing some of the glass, but every time they did, German shells came. The relentless artillery bombardment continues, with 3,000 shells falling on or near the Cathedral within a 24-hour period, yet the structure endures. The German forces use shrapnel, rather than high-explosive shells, in their attack, making it clear that they wish to torment, but not destroy the Cathedral. It is a futile gesture—a vain attempt to break something unbreakable.

When I first arrived at the Cathedral, I was told that there had been a few days of calm. But upon my return the next morning, five more shells had landed in the vicinity. I saw firsthand the damage caused by a 155-mm shell that exploded at the base of the eastern wall. I had been there the evening before, and the hole certainly wasn't there then. I inspected it at 8:20 a.m., just two hours after it had been created, and a newspaper boy was offering me the morning's paper right next to it. The wreckage from the shelling was fresh, but the Cathedral, remarkably, remained standing.

Later that day, we had lunch in a hotel in Rheims, which had recently reopened after a period of closure. The landlady and her relative served us, both still in mourning.

Despite the recent shelling, the atmosphere in the hotel was oddly calm. The women moved through the destruction with a stoic indifference, continuing to serve their guests with professionalism, as though nothing had happened. Their composure in the face of such devastation was inspiring. Outside, the sun shone, and life—though altered—seemed to go on. Dogs played in the streets, and children wandered beneath the trees. Even though the city was battered, the resilience of its people was evident.

During lunch, several officers joined us—men who had fought through the battles of the Marne and the Aisne, and through the trenches. Despite their terrifying experiences, none had been wounded. They spoke with great sophistication and calm about the horrors they had witnessed, but they also expressed their admiration for the bravery and heroism of the French soldiers and civilians. One officer shared a story about a soldier who, when caught in the open between enemy lines, continued to shout "Vive la France!" despite being repeatedly shot. His courage was unyielding, even as his body was riddled with bullets.

After the meal, we continued our journey through the war-torn countryside, passing through towns and fields that had been transformed by the war. Everything around us seemed to be in service to the conflict, even the most mundane activities. And yet, amid the destruction, there were moments of strange beauty—an orchard blooming under a bright sun, or a tree-lined path leading us forward, toward the unknown. As we neared Arras, the war's presence was undeniable, yet life—somehow—continued, in spite of it all.

When you finally arrive in Arras, there is no mistaking the extent of the devastation that has befallen the city. Unlike

Rheims, which offers a fleeting illusion of its former self, Arras reveals its true state immediately. The first street you encounter is a scene of utter desolation, empty and foreboding. Grimy curtains hang in tattered sheets, bulging out from shattered windows. Everywhere you look, the remnants of shellfire are evident. Bits and pieces of buildings are strewn across the roads and pavements, interspersed with patches of grass growing where once there were homes. As you continue through the city, you reach a large circular square, which was once grand but now lies in ruin. Every building surrounding it is in the same sorry condition, and there is an eerie silence that hangs in the air. In the brief moments between the thunderous cannon fire, the only sound that breaks the silence is the rustling of blinds and curtains fluttering against the empty window frames, or the faint, idle banging of a loose shutter. Not a single cat wanders the streets. We are utterly alone, accompanied only by a small group of staff officers, our reluctant guides through this war-torn landscape. We cannot shake the feeling that we are intruders, desecrating a place that was once full of life.

Across from us, a shell has struck a house, tearing off its entire front. Through the gaping hole, we can see the drawing-room on the ground floor and, above it, the bedroom. The bed is neatly made, the white linens still pristine, as if it were untouched by the chaos outside. Strangely, everything remains eerily still. The furniture, despite the slope of the floor, has not yet toppled into the street below. The bedroom looks like a display in a museum, as though it is a famous person's bedroom on display for tourists—untouched, preserved, yet so far removed from its original function. Outside, a few chairs have been knocked out of the house and lie upside down in the street, among the debris, left undisturbed. In every direction, streets branch off, but they are silent and overrun with grass and ruin.

"See the fortress I have here!" says the Commanding Officer with bitter irony. "Notice its strategic importance. It's open on every side. You can walk right in, as if it were a windmill. And still, they bomb it. Yesterday, they fired twenty shells every minute for an hour into the city. Completely pointless destruction. But that's how they are!"

We move further into the city, and the scenes grow even stranger. One house is reduced to nothing but a roof, which now forms a sort of triumphal arch. All around, potted plants—still blooming—are either boxed against walls or hanging from window frames. The streets are covered in a fine layer of powdered glass. Telephone and telegraph wires hang in thick, tangled strands, reminiscent of abandoned spider webs, often blocking your path and forcing you to dodge them. The sounds of things shifting or falling inside the ruined buildings are constant, creating an eerie atmosphere. Then, suddenly, a sound pierces the silence—the cry of a baby. It's a stark reminder that the city, despite the destruction, is not entirely abandoned. A woman emerges from her house, carefully locking the door behind her. Is she securing it against the threat of shells or to keep out thieves? As we walk, we notice pipes emerging from the pavement, emitting blue smoke. These pipes are the outward sign that the few remaining inhabitants have converted their cellars into makeshift living spaces—drawing-rooms and bedrooms that offer some semblance of safety.

We descend into one such underground refuge. The ground-floor drawing-room, with its fine furniture, has been devastated by a shell, mixing rich carvings with pieces of shattered walls and curtains under a layer of dust. But the underground quarters, with their sturdy arched roof and solid appearance, are well-organized, neat, and surprisingly cozy, offering a modicum of comfort amid the chaos. The entrance is carefully protected, shielding the inhabitants from further bombardment.

"Still," says the homeowner with a shrug, "a 210-mm shell would go through everything. That would be the end of us." He raises his hands in resignation, his fatalism almost matching that of the city itself—a place with a long history of suffering. Arras has been besieged and ravaged countless times. The original Vandals attacked it repeatedly, followed by the Franks, the Normans in the ninth century, and various other invaders. In the fifteenth century, Charles VI laid siege to it for seven weeks without success, and under Louis XI, it was brutally mistreated. In the end, it fell under Spanish rule, only to be regained by France in 1640 after another siege. Since then, the city has had relatively quiet periods, save for the Revolution and, of course, the current devastation. Those who have remained here seem to have inherited a remarkable capacity to endure suffering.

In the street where we first noticed the stove-pipes rising from the pavement, a postman appears, dressed in the standard French postal uniform, with the familiar black wallet-box hanging from his waist and a pen behind his ear. He moves from house to house, delivering letters in a manner that would seem ordinary in any other city—except here, he simply slides the letters through the empty window frames, never knocking. It's a striking image, both ordinary and surreal, a testament to the persistence of life amid ruin.

We continue our journey and arrive at the Cathedral of St. Vaast, an imposing structure in the city that stands out even in its ruined state. Though not highly praised by architectural critics, Arras Cathedral's massive, simple baroque style makes it a perfect candidate for bearing the brunt of bombardment. Its vast, flat surfaces have absorbed countless blows, but the building's strength remains. The scars from the shelling are plainly visible, yet they do not diminish the grandeur of the Cathedral. If anything, they add to its somber beauty, making it a symbol of religious devotion amid destruction. German commanders who have bombarded this site have only contributed to the Cathedral's tragic magnificence. Despite the devastation, the Cathedral's presence is both majestic and haunting, far more striking than the famous Cathedral of Rheims.

In the north transept, a 325-mm shell has created a gaping hole large enough to allow a giant creature to pass through. Yet, even in the midst of this wreckage, there is an incredible juxtaposition—nearby, a café remains almost untouched. The glasses, mugs, and chairs still sit there, covered in dust, exactly as they were left. You could easily reach through a window to retrieve a glass, yet the scene is absurdly still, as if the city had been frozen in time. Nearby, an old house shows off its exposed rafters, while a beam has fallen from the ceiling, now burning in the open air, consumed by flames.

Despite the destruction, life persists. Further along, we come across a greengrocer's shop, still open and operating, offering a strange semblance of normalcy in an otherwise devastated world. As we circle around the Cathedral and reach the Town Hall, we encounter more ruins. Built in the sixteenth century and carefully restored in the nineteenth, the Town Hall now lies in ruins. Behind it, an abandoned automobile, overrun with rust, serves as a sad symbol of the surrounding desolation. The vehicle, untouched by time, stands silent amid the ongoing war, a poignant reminder of the city's quiet suffering.

To the right of the Town Hall, we come upon a strange sight—rows of mounds of bricks, stones, and debris. These mounds have no resemblance to homes, or even anything recognizably human. They are simply piles of rubble, marking the remains of what was once the city's most important street. The street, full of life and commerce, is gone, its character erased by relentless bombardment. It may eventually be rebuilt, but it will never be the same.

Curious, I ask, "What's the name of this street?"

None of the officers in the group could recall the name of the main business street in Arras, and there wasn't a single local in sight to ask. It was as though the very name of the street had vanished, as if erased from memory, much like the buildings that had once stood there. Despite searching for it in travel guides, encyclopedias, and maps, it remained elusive—lost to history, hidden somewhere deep in time.

The street's devastation wasn't its own misfortune; it was simply in the path of the German artillery aimed at the Town Hall. The destruction it endured was a byproduct of a military focus that had nothing to do with the street itself, but rather the Town Hall, which became the primary target. The Germans had no military interest in the Town Hall—it held no strategic value. However, it was the grandest structure in Arras, beloved by the locals, irreplaceable in its charm. This made it a symbolic target. It felt as though, instead of aiming directly at the Town Hall, the Germans were indirectly attacking it by inflicting harm on everything around it, as if holding a soldier's child hostage and threatening to maim it unless the soldier surrendered. Whether this action was a result of military logic or sheer madness, it was a deliberate attack on something that meant so much to the people.

Upon reaching the front of the Town Hall, we could fully see how much the Germans had concentrated their efforts on it. The Town Hall sat at the edge of a vast and impressive arcaded square, its uniform architecture unmistakably from the time of the Spanish occupation. As we looked at this square, and its nearly identical twin just a short distance away, it became clear that Arras was once a noble city, full of grandeur. Remarkably, the square itself had barely been touched by the shelling. There were no shells wasted on the square, for the Germans had concentrated all their fire on the Town Hall, ensuring that the more valuable structure remained in ruins.

From the far side of the square, I stood under the arcade to shield myself from the rain and sketched a rough outline of the ruined Town Hall. When I compared my sketch with an old engraving of the same scene, the destruction became even more apparent. The ground-floor colonnade had some arches still standing, their outlines intact, but the upper part of the facade was reduced to rubble, with only a fragment of a wall remaining, revealing two window holes. The entire roof was gone, and the later addition to the left of the building had been completely wiped out. The earlier, carved masonry to the right of the Town Hall was still standing but severely damaged. The once proud belfry, which had been the tallest in France at nearly 250 feet, was gone. What remained was a jagged stump, like the broken tooth of a giant, stubbornly reaching a few feet higher than the original roofline. Around the ruins, piles of refuse and debris created a grim scene.

Arras, let it be remembered, is in France, not Germany. This fact is significant because, at the time, Germany was supposedly fighting a defensive war, protecting its borders and upholding what it considered the highest ideals of civilization. Yet, here we were, in Arras, a French city, which had suffered a level of destruction unparalleled by anything in Germany. The Germans had advanced through Belgium and into France, not to conquer, but to "defend" themselves. And in doing so, they obliterated the beauty of Arras, turning it into an unrecognizable wasteland, all in the name of preserving their own civilization. It's difficult to comprehend how the Germans could justify such actions if they were truly defending their homes. What would have happened, one wonders, had they been waging a war of conquest and destruction? Would they have gone further?

I am not a proponent of revenge or retaliation, but it is hard to ignore the harsh reality. Germany must understand the full extent of the destruction it has caused. The best way for them to grasp this would be if, at the end of the war, one of their own cities—say, Cologne—were left in a similar state to that of Arras. This might be harsh on Cologne, but it would not be any more severe than what Arras had endured. Moreover, it is widely believed that the hardships of war bring out the best in a nation's character. If this is true, then war, with all its suffering, is somehow a necessary evil. Yet, having seen the devastation in Arras, I cannot deny that I would, without hesitation, trade a year's income to see Cologne reduced to the same state. This desire, though perhaps unjustifiable, stems from seeing firsthand the utter destruction of a place once filled with life and beauty.

As we continued our journey through the city, we passed street after street where not a single building remained intact or inhabited. These streets, at first glance, appeared to be silent, as though the residents were indoors, waiting for the turmoil to pass. But there was no one indoors. There was no one at all. The entire neighborhood was deserted, a ghost town. The solitude was oppressive and unsettling. Every window was shattered, every wall was chipped, and entire sections of some buildings had been completely knocked out. One building revealed its six rooms, each exposed to the elements, with the once-fine wallpaper now crumbling away. The owner of this place had an apparent fondness for anthracite stoves, as each of the six fireplaces contained one, all miraculously undamaged. The post office had been obliterated, reduced to a pile of rubble.

Next, we came to the railway station, built by the Compagnie du Nord in 1898, a relatively modern structure. Its façade was impressive, but now it was pockmarked by shell holes of all sizes. A shell had narrowly missed the station's ornate front, scraping off some of the decorations. Every pane of glass was shattered, and the ironwork was covered in a thick layer of rust. The station's signs, which would normally guide passengers, were eerily still. You could look straight through the station as if it were an empty skeleton. The silence within, punctuated only by the distant sound of artillery, was unnatural, chilling. On the platforms, the glass shelters for passengers were smashed into tiny fragments, the ironwork now coated in rust. The signal posts stood desolate and forlorn, their purpose rendered meaningless by the wreckage. Even the railway tracks themselves were overtaken by rampant vegetation, a jungle creeping across the rails. This, we were told, was the result of Germany's defensive war—a war fought to protect the homeland and its supposed ideals. The reality, however, was a city transformed into an eerie ruin, a testament to the devastating cost of war. This scene unfolded on July 7th, 1915, a day that will remain etched in the memory of all who witnessed it.

IV At Grips

Earlier, I have mentioned the seemingly vague and casual nature of war when it is conducted on a scale so vast that it becomes almost unfathomable. When you are with a Staff officer, you are able to observe almost everything firsthand. While I am certain there are certain matters kept hidden from you, by and large, you are given access to nearly all that is visible. Of course, there is no possibility of peering into the General's mind, which holds the key to the strategies that will shape the course of history. The General may talk at length about the past or the present, offering insightful reflections. But when it comes to the future, he remains tight-lipped. If he is positioned near the center of the front, he might tell you, in his calm manner, that a significant movement might be expected on the wings. Conversely, if he is stationed at one of the wings, he will assure you, just as blandly, that a major movement may soon unfold at the center. You do not feel disappointed by such responses, for you know that the questions you pose deserve precisely such answers. Yet, despite this, there is an unmistakable sense of disappointment in being unable to grasp even the present moment—the overwhelming events unfolding around you, pounding in your ears, and blurring your vision.

Take, for instance, the sound of guns. I am not referring to the persistent, almost continuous rumble of gunfire that seems to echo from every direction, but rather the particular sound of a specific cluster of guns. I inquire about them, and at times, even the Staff officers hesitate before deciding whether they belong to the enemy or the French forces. Generally, a civilian can distinguish an enemy shot by the terrifying, whizzing sound of the projectile as it rushes toward him. On the other hand, a

French shell, rushing away from him, falls silent before the noise of the explosion has even reached his ears. I might find myself caught in between a group of German guns and a group of French guns, nearly equidistant from both.

Once I have been informed about the type of guns and their caliber, and perhaps even the rough location of these weapons on the Staff map, I realize that this knowledge brings me no closer to understanding the full scope of the situation. To actually locate these guns might take half a day's effort, and even when I do find them, I discover nothing more than a few pieces of machinery tucked away in a makeshift shelter, operating in isolation with the assistance of a few sweat-drenched men. The process is far removed from the image of warfare that one might expect. A sleek projectile is loaded into the gun, followed by a deafening blast—and the projectile vanishes, leaving no trace. No one in the shelter seems concerned with where it went or what it did. A telephone sits nearby, but all that emanates from it are numbers, technical jargon, and, occasionally, a reprimand, prompting the sweating men to make minor adjustments to the gun or the next round of ammunition.

I have no understanding of the target, and neither do the men operating the guns. I am free to venture out in search of the target. It is pointed out to me. Perhaps it is a building or a group of structures, or it might be something entirely different. At best, it is nothing more than a distant speck in the sprawling, complicated terrain. From my vantage point, I observe a faint puff of smoke, as delicate and harmless as a feather drifting through the air. In that moment, I cannot help but wonder: Can anyone truly expect these men, operating their noisy contraption in an enclosed hut far behind the lines, to accurately target that tiny, far-off red mark on the distant structure? And even if, by some miracle, they manage to strike it, what significance does that particular target hold in the grand scheme of the conflict? What impact could its destruction possibly have on the broader course of the war? This is where war feels inexplicably vague and disconnected, because even a mere fragment of it is beyond comprehension, and the individual parts of that fragment fail to fit together into any coherent whole. I recall standing in a front-line trench, listening to the furious gunfire all around me, and yet seeing nothing, understanding nothing of the battle unfolding in the distance.

The same sense of disconnection applies to the movements of troops. For instance, I was once sleeping in a town behind the frontlines when I was abruptly woken not by the usual roar of an airplane overhead, but by an intense shaking and rumbling of the hotel itself. This tremor persisted for a long stretch of time, from just after dawn until about six o'clock, only to begin again shortly after. I rose from my bed and ventured outside, only to find that the entire town was shaking and vibrating. A regiment was passing through, traveling in buses. Each bus held around thirty soldiers, and the buses followed one another at intervals of no more than thirty yards. The buses, painted in a dull gray resembling battleships, were nearly identical, except for the fact that some had permanent roofs, while others had only temporary ones. Some featured mica windows, while others had open holes in the sides. All of the buses carried the same number of soldiers, and in each, the rifles were stacked in precisely the same manner. When one bus came to a halt, all the others did the same. The soldiers waved and smiled at the young women standing at the windows or in the streets. The whole town was awakening. No matter how early one rises in such towns, the day has already begun for everyone else.

The soldiers, dressed in their pale-blue uniforms, appeared young, energetic, and somewhat worn from their travels. Their faces, their mustaches, their hair, and even their ears were coated with a thick layer of dust. Clearly, they had been on the move for hours. The buses kept emerging from the dusty haze at the far end of town, and they disappeared around the corner near the Town Hall. Occasionally, an officer's car or a vehicle carrying a couple of nurses would pass by, briefly interrupting the procession, but soon the buses continued, one after another. The impression left was that the entire French Army was marching through the town. The noise, the vibrations, the rattling—everything seemed to reverberate in my nerves. Finally, two breakdown trucks passed, and the procession seemed to come to a halt. I couldn't quite believe that it was really over, but the silence that followed was almost overwhelming.

What I had witnessed were just two regiments passing through the town—out of the hundreds that made up the French Army. Two regiments! Yet no one could tell me where they had come from, what their mission had been, where they were going, or what their specific role was in the broader plan of battle. They moved with an air of aimlessness, much like a flock of birds soaring across a vast landscape.

But among the various movements, there were more poignant scenes. One of the most striking and moving sights I encountered at the front was the march of a regiment into a small country town on a bright, beautiful summer morning. First came the regimental band, its brass instruments tarnished and battered, with the musicians carrying odd packages tied to their backpacks. These were not just musicians, but soldiers as well, dressed in worn and dirty uniforms. Despite their obvious fatigue, they marched with a certain dignity, playing a lively tune. Following them were cyclists, keeping pace with the marching troops. Then came an officer on horseback, followed by the main body of the regiment. Many of the rifles had their stocks wrapped in ragged cloth. Each soldier carried whatever they had managed to bring with them to the campaign, including a pair of field glasses. The men were burdened with an assortment of broken, torn, and patched-up gear. Their exhaustion was evident in every step, their faces pale and drawn. Among them was a young officer who seemed barely able to walk, as if each step took everything out of him. He moved as though in a trance, his movements slow and laborious, perhaps from sheer exhaustion. Occasionally, a triangular flag would be raised to signal the positions of different companies in the trenches. The regiment had come from the trenches, though which ones, no one could say.

What followed was a procession of logistical support: Red Cross units, horses, field kitchens, carts, machine-guns, and ammunition. Steam rose from the cooking equipment as meals were prepared. Even in the midst of war, the regiment seemed self-sufficient, managing its own food, medical supplies, and ammunition without fanfare or ceremony. The march was not a grand review, but the quiet, determined rhythm of a fighting force enduring the hardships of war.

As the regiment passed by, I couldn't help but feel a sense of deep empathy for those soldiers. I wished for that young officer to find a place to rest, a decent bed where he could recover from his fatigue. It was a scene full of pathos, yet shrouded in mystery. What was the role of this particular regiment in the larger strategy devised by General Joffre?

Despite all this, after some time at the front, one begins to understand that, while the conduct of the war may seem mysterious, it is neither vague nor casual. I recall visiting a recently liberated village, still bearing the marks of its recent conquest. The soldiers I encountered were full of energy, but there was an unmistakable sense of alertness in their demeanor. They were constantly on guard, acutely aware of the dangers surrounding them. As we explored the village, it became clear that everything had been meticulously organized: trenches, strongholds, machine guns, barbed wire—all designed to withstand enemy attacks. The Commandant, visibly anxious, made sure we were safely out of sight from potential German snipers, knowing that any lapse in vigilance could result in catastrophic consequences.

A path had been carved through an entire row of cottages, allowing us to move along it. It felt like walking through a lane lined with silent, watchful figures. Then, a hushed voice warned us not to speak, as the Germans might overhear. We proceeded cautiously, peering into deep mines, crawling through narrow passages, and vanishing into long underground tunnels. We emerged into a space where soldiers stood, cheerfully eating while chatting among themselves. Nearby, a group of men practiced with harmless hand grenades, their explosions reverberating in the air.

I followed the Commandant as we turned a corner and found ourselves gazing at something—though I no longer remember what it was. "Don't stay here," he said, motioning for me to move along. Almost as soon as I stepped away, a bullet struck the wall where I had been standing just seconds before. It was a stark reminder of the constant danger lurking around every corner.

The atmosphere at the front was charged with tension. There was an overwhelming sense that everyone was locked in a continuous struggle, pushing against one another like wrestlers, every inch of ground hotly contested. "Casual" would be the last word one would use to describe anything happening here.

On another occasion, after a lengthy walk, one of the staff captains instructed a car to meet us at the end of a road. Part of this road was exposed to German artillery from several miles away. No sooner had the car appeared than we heard the unmistakable, sinister sound of an incoming shell. It sliced through the air, and before the sizzling sound even faded, the explosion echoed through the landscape. The shell—a 77mm high-explosive—landed with a thunderous roar.

The Germans were methodical in their shelling. For the next half hour, they meticulously pounded the same stretch of road, releasing shell after shell at intervals of two minutes. Each shell fell at regular distances, every hundred yards along the slope. From a nearby dugout, I observed the bombardment. It was a chilling demonstration of the Germans' precision, though, from my perspective, it also seemed like a foolish waste of ammunition. The road was clearly empty, and yet they continued to fire.

Naturally, we decided not to use that road. Instead, we took a detour through a wooded area to meet the car at a safer location. The road was inevitable, however, as it was the only route available. The Commandant, ever the professional, was unmoved by the dangers. "The car must go up the road," he declared, undeterred. "Let it go."

The fact that the car was being used for civilian convenience rather than military operations didn't concern him. It was still a military vehicle, driven by a soldier, and it had a job to do. His words were almost playful as he turned to the chauffeur: "You may as well go right away. We will watch you suffer!" A subordinate officer chuckled at the situation, though I could see he was concerned.

Despite our reservations, the car went ahead. The shelling eventually stopped, and the chauffeur made it through unscathed, reporting back later that five large craters had formed in the road.

Another time, we found ourselves in the trenches, making our way through a labyrinth of narrow, winding communication trenches on a steep slope. A careless moment—a brief exposure above the trench's parapet—resulted in an immediate bombardment of high-explosive shells. At that moment, exhaustion from our trek, along with a gnawing hunger, seemed to vanish. The sound of shells whistling overhead snapped me to attention, and suddenly all fatigue faded into the background.

The shells continued to fall in our vicinity, growing progressively closer. We split into pairs and ran, keeping a distance between us, as per instructions. After each explosion, we would pause, counting five seconds, until all fragments of the shell had settled. It wasn't long before a shell seemed to drop directly in front of me, causing the ground to shake violently. I felt the sting of the explosion's fumes, but it had not landed directly on me—it had fallen just to my left.

Trenches, I realized, were marvels of survival. I felt the shockwave of the blast, but the trench had shielded me. Moments later, a friend picked up a piece of shrapnel from the shell—a jagged, multifaceted ball that was designed to cause maximum damage. It was a sobering reminder that, even in the face of such chaos, war was neither casual nor accidental.

One of the places where the brutal, unyielding nature of war was made most apparent to me was at Notre Dame de Lorette. The little chapel that stood there, now an iconic symbol of the war, was far from beautiful, at least according to the photographs. But the ground around it was another matter. The land behind the frontlines was meticulously organized, with layers of defenses both above and below ground, designed to withstand the violence of warfare. While the layout of the area remains unspoken, I can tell you that it included every kind of precaution, from supplies stored safely underground to various types of defensive strategies.

I remember seeing stacks of lamp-chimneys buried in the earth, untouched by time. The scene was hauntingly complete, an embodiment of the thoroughness with which war was prepared for. Among these, we encountered prisoners—two young German soldiers under guard in a small cabin. They had wandered too far into the maze of trenches and had lost their way. One of them was a Red Cross man, likely a medical student before the war. He was dusty, tired, and seemed to bear the weight of a mission he no longer believed in. I found myself sympathetic towards him. His face, though weary and grim, still held a trace of youthful strength.

We soon encountered another prisoner, a boy no older than twenty-one. He was ill, covered in dirt, his uniform in tatters, stained by blood and bullet holes. Someone had given him a hunk of bread, stuffed inside his tunic. He looked a shadow of his former self, hollow-eyed and spent. The officer in charge questioned him, but the boy had little to say. His spirits seemed broken, but there was an undeniable relief in his demeanor, as if, at long last, he was free from the horrors of war. I couldn't help but wonder about the woman who had sent him off to fight—perhaps his mother. Her heartbreak was unimaginable, and yet, in the context of the war, she would have been told that her son had died for a noble cause.

Later, as we moved on from the prisoners and their grim stories, we came across something more strategic—a map. This map was immense, spread out in the middle of a forest clearing. Using different colored chalks, it marked the progress of the frontlines, with yellow showing the advance up to May, blue marking further gains in June, and red indicating the latest encroachments, just the previous night.

The officers surveyed the map with pride, pointing out key positions. Their voices, filled with determination, spoke of where the next battles would unfold. The map was a testament to the relentless pressure being applied to the Germans. Though they respected the enemy's military prowess, the officers here held a particular contempt for certain German divisions, particularly the Prussians, whom they considered to be less resilient than the Bavarians.

Beyond the wood, the landscape was a wasteland. The ground had been bombarded relentlessly, leaving behind nothing but craters and twisted metal. There were no trees, no vegetation—just desolation. The communication trenches we followed led us through this barren land, where not a single blade of grass could grow. The endless shelling had sterilized the earth.

As we continued our journey, we met soldiers who told us their stories. One Captain recounted how, on March 9th, he and his men had fought to hold their position despite the freezing water and ice in the trench. "We didn't surrender," he said proudly, "but we lost twenty men and twenty-four more had frostbitten feet." For him, that date had marked a turning point in his life.

Further along, we came across another officer urgently speaking into a telephone, directing his men on where to fire. All around us, the war was unfolding in real-time, with soldiers still engaged in the fight for ground that seemed to slip through their fingers.

Then, we reached a spot where we could see the plains. Ruined villages, devastated by the conflict, dotted the landscape. Souchez, St. Eloi, Angres—names now infamous across the globe for the bloodshed they had witnessed. The village of Ablain St. Nazaire, though, stood out. Once a thriving community, it was now little more than a collection of blackened timbers and shattered structures. Its church, a hollow shell, rose like a skeletal remains. For those soldiers who had fought and died there, this village would never be the same again.

V. British Lines

Imagine a vast plain, but not an empty one. Nor is it a barren stretch devoid of life or elevation. Rather, it's a landscape dotted with hills, among which rises a particularly notable one, crowned by a charming old town that offers sweeping views of the surrounding area. This expanse is far from monotonous. It is richly wooded, well cultivated, and by no means desolate. The plain is alive with villages scattered across it, and small market towns are never too far apart. These settlements are interconnected by a network of roads, many paved, and canals, with a respectable number of railways threading through them.

From an aerial view, the first thing that stands out is the abundance of trees. Their rounded tops seem to dominate the landscape, and only the tops of church towers rise above this verdant canopy. Other forms of architecture are less prominent, visible only in glimpses between the foliage. The landscape's predominant hues are shades of green and grey, and often the sky mirrors this palette, heavy and overcast. The stark contrast between Northern France and Southern Belgium is subtle, marked only by the language on shop signs and café menus, with the two regions otherwise bearing a striking resemblance in their physical and cultural characteristics.

The British presence in this land is notable, distinguished by a blend of formal civility and underlying warmth. The occupation is both conspicuous and discreet, a balance of military order and human connection.

One particular encounter stands out. As I sat in a village street, enjoying an outdoor meal of jam sandwiches, with a motorcar serving as our buffet, I asked a scruffy young boy playing with a small terrier, "What do you call your dog?"

He responded with a shy but proud smile, "Tommy." The countryside, criss-crossed by telegraph and telephone lines, teems with a visible sense of structure, not least in the form of road signs. The signs are large and direct, one of the most common being the command to "Motor-lorries dead slow," displayed in bold letters against the backdrop of foreign streets. At nearly every busy intersection in the towns, soldiers stand as traffic directors, ensuring the smooth flow of an impressive volume of vehicles.

The roads are constantly congested, teeming with mechanical transport. The sheer scale of traffic is overwhelming, with motor-lorries monopolizing the roads. These enormous vehicles, with their ungainly size, create chaos when they become tangled with other forms of transport—motor-cars, despatch riders on motorcycles, peasant carts, and marching soldiers. The result is a traffic jam far more chaotic than one might find in a bustling city center, such as Piccadilly Circus before a theatre show. The motor-lorries, though cumbersome, often contribute to the gridlock not just due to their sheer size, but because of the behavior of the soldiers riding on them. Each motor-lorry typically carries two soldiers at the front and one at the back. However, the solitary soldier at the rear, feeling isolated, often jumps to the front seat to join his comrades, creating a bottleneck behind them as other vehicles desperately try to navigate past. Only when a Staff officer's car is affected do the soldiers begrudgingly return to their proper seats, following a brief but sharp reprimand.

This bustling, disordered activity on the roads paints a picture of an intricate, well-oiled machine operating in the background. It's a system so vast and multifaceted that it immediately calls to mind the one man who is the central figure in this organization—the supreme commander. Though he is not elusive, his presence looms large. Word spreads quickly that he will be available to meet at a certain time, and when you arrive a few minutes ahead of schedule, you find yourself in a large, somewhat austere office with a distinctly Gallic flair, softened by the heavy presence of his Anglo-Saxon staff.

You are soon introduced to the members of the General Staff, who, though famous and renowned, walk in and out of the office with an air of casual indifference. They are experts, their names synonymous with military excellence, but in the next room, beyond the heavy double doors, sits the true power of this operation. The Commander-in-Chief. When you are finally allowed into his presence, the effect is immediate—a sense of awe and gravity fills the room.

The room itself, once a drawing room, still carries hints of its former elegance, with silk-paneled walls and the lingering presence of a grand piano in the corner. In the center, a large table holds a detailed map, stretching across the table like a landscape in miniature. The man himself is a thick-set figure, not tall but solid, with small hands and feet, his nails worn with character. His short white mustache and light eyes contrast sharply with his ruddy complexion. His chin is particularly noticeable, an almost defiant feature. There's nothing overly refined about him; instead, his demeanor is focused and intense, speaking in short, reflective sentences, and walking back and forth, pausing thoughtfully between words. When he speaks about the enemy, particularly the Germans, there's a deliberate gesture, a defiant shake of the head that speaks volumes of his resolve. It's the posture of a man ready to settle old scores. His presence exudes an air of dogged determination and quiet pugnacity.

After a brief conversation, the Commander-in-Chief dismisses you, and as you leave, the feeling of having met a legendary figure lingers. But he is not the only figure of importance in this sprawling military network. There are two other key figures, both equally formidable in their own right: the Quartermaster-General, who oversees the supply of materials, and the Adjutant-General, responsible for the supply of manpower. Alongside him is the Grand Provost Marshal, a figure of ultimate authority, ensuring discipline and upholding the power to determine life and death.

Each of these figures operates within a network that spans across multiple layers of command. Every army, corps, division, and brigade has its own leader and staff, all working tirelessly to ensure the smooth functioning of this vast and complex military operation. During my time in the field, I had the opportunity to dine and converse with several high-ranking officers, all of whom were admirably dedicated and constantly on the move. They rarely had time to relax, with some rising at dawn and retiring only after midnight. One general I met remarked on his beautiful garden, but when I asked if he ever visited it, he replied with a wry smile, "I have never been into it."

In the evenings, after a long day's work, the generals often departed in their limousines, heading back to their offices for the late-night session of work that would stretch until the early hours of the morning. The sheer volume of work and responsibility at even the lowest level of command, such as a Divisional Headquarters, is staggering. Each division commands around twenty thousand soldiers, and the work involved is largely administrative, often mundane and routine. However, some of the most fascinating work occurs in the photography and map-making departments. Thousands of maps are produced, each one showing a different aspect of the battlefield at various points in time, and special maps are regularly circulated to field officers, ensuring they have the most up-to-date information to guide their decisions.

In every corner of this vast network, from the generals to the foot soldiers, there is a relentless focus on order, precision, and efficiency, reflecting the immense responsibility borne by each individual in maintaining the war effort.

The Royal Flying Corps' fitting-out and repair sheds were some of the most remarkable structures I had ever seen—perfectly designed, not only for their practical purpose but also with a touch of elegance. I had the opportunity to visit them during a fierce storm, which only heightened the sense of awe. The machinery inside was vast and impressive; the production levels, staggering. The organization was methodical, scientific, and efficient, and the staff, both friendly and highly capable. As I looked at the planes—those birdcages full of birds, as they were often called—and absorbed the very essence of flight, it was no longer hard to imagine the extraordinary feats these airmen were performing daily, soaring through the skies in all directions. One man, for example, flew over Ghent twice a week as regularly as a train schedule and had never been seriously harmed. These aviators had a unique physical advantage, or so it was believed—the noise of their own engine drowned out the sounds of the shrapnel explosions aimed at them.

The British soldier stationed in France and Flanders, it turns out, is far from self-sufficient. He requires an incredible amount of support—more than most could imagine. I once saw the rations for a single day laid out on a tray, and it seemed like an impossible amount of food to consume in just one sitting. There was meat, abundant bacon, cheese, jam, bread, and vegetables. There were also tea, sugar, salt, condiments, and sometimes butter, as well as a weekly supply of two ounces of tobacco and a box of matches. But the most prominent item on the tray was undoubtedly the meat. Alongside this, the soldier needed more than just food. He needed fuel, letters from loved ones, cleanliness, clothing, and an array of war supplies that were necessary for daily survival and warfare. And all of these needs had to be met, consistently, with great precision.

The magnitude of this demand can only be grasped when you consider the continuous streams of goods arriving in Northern France, not only from Britain but from across the world. This flow of materials, driven by the urgency of the war, is like a powerful, unrelenting force—an invisible magnet pulling everything towards the frontlines, day and night. Tracking the specific path or the precise contents of these streams would be nearly impossible, but there is one point where all of them converge: the railhead.

A military railhead might seem like an unremarkable, average little railway station, but it is, in fact, a crucial hub. It's not even the end of a railway line, though it serves as the headquarters for a Divisional Supply Column—a division that is just one among many in France and Flanders. This particular station was run by a Major, who, despite his khaki uniform and his use of military language, was not like the stereotypical regimental Major. His focus was not on strategy or combat but on the business of supply. His job was to receive orders from the Brigades of the Division, which changed constantly, and to ensure those orders were fulfilled within a tight window of thirty-six hours. It's possible this Major had never even seen a trench, and he certainly wasn't skilled with a revolver, but his expertise lay in handling the logistical aspects of war—making sure the trains arrived on time and that the lorries were in perfect working order. His team's honor was bound up in receipts, not battle strategies.

This Major was responsible for everything his division needed, except for water and ammunition. He oversaw the arrival of trains loaded with supplies, ranging from food and clothing to field kitchens and field guns, even receiving letters from soldiers' wives. He never questioned how these items arrived; his sole concern was ensuring the trains were punctual and that his motor-lorries were in top condition. Day after day, tons of supplies poured out from the railhead under his watchful eye, including 280 bags of mail sent to the troops on the front lines. His vehicles were maintained with such precision that they gleamed as if they were the engines of a luxury yacht. It was, in a way, the dandyism of the Army Service Corps, but it was also vital to the smooth operation of the war effort.

An integral part of the railhead operation was the Railway Construction Section Train, which could lay new track at an astounding rate—several miles a day. This self-contained train served as a depot, a workshop, and a barracks all in one, ensuring the continued expansion and maintenance of the railway lines that connected the front lines to the rest of the world.

As I traveled along the roads, I occasionally saw rough signs nailed to trees with labels such as "Forage," "Groceries," "Meat," and "Bread." If I waited long enough, I could watch one of the streams of motor-lorries from the railhead pull over and unload their cargo. Within moments, the supplies—be it meat, bread, or vegetables—would vanish as quickly as they had appeared, spirited away to the camps, billets, and trenches. In another part of the field, I might witness frozen mutton from New Zealand being roasted in an earth oven, a sight that, though somewhat rustic, was strangely satisfying. The sheer amount of food being prepared was staggering, and it struck me as remarkable how even in such a primitive setup, so much could be done.

Beyond the food supplies, there were the non-edible materials, especially in the engineer's park. There, you would find every conceivable tool and device related to warfare—things that were often too complex to describe in detail but were essential to the war effort. The telephones, helmets, and other pieces of equipment were beyond anything most civilians had ever seen. And then, there was the ammunition train—a truly terrifying sight. Unloading that train meant handling every kind of ammunition, from rifle cartridges to massive shells that could easily destroy vehicles. Alongside the explosives, there were various pyrotechnic devices and bombs, some of which seemed like they were just waiting for the slightest touch to set them off. The officers handled these devices with unsettling nonchalance, as though they were merely routine items, but it was hard not to feel a sense of danger in their presence.

The most remarkable thing, however, was the absence of the soldiers themselves. In the British lines, it was almost as if the Army itself was invisible. You could see soldiers everywhere, but they were usually engaged in supporting roles, ensuring that the material needs of other soldiers were met. The actual fighters were harder to find, often in small groups or single units. On one particularly long walk through the countryside, I accompanied a General and tramped through trenches, only to discover two soldiers—an officer and his subordinate. But even they weren't on the front lines. The officer spent his days observing the German front through a telescope from his dug-out, where he had a bed, a telephone, and a few personal items. Occasionally, the telephone would buzz faintly, but when I asked about it, the orderly explained that it was nothing to worry about. It was only someone talking to someone else.

The officer's task was to monitor a specific section of the front and report on it, but as I stood there, I couldn't help but think of the vast expanse of land, the hills and dales we had crossed to get to this point, and the seemingly trivial patches of earth that had been the focus of so much violence. It made me wonder how much blood had been spilled for such small and insignificant pieces of land.

The officer meticulously explained every detail to us, providing an in-depth understanding of the German soldiers' behavior, as he had observed them. Yet, when it came to his own habits, he remained silent. He wasn't just an officer; he was a mere observer—constantly watching through a narrow slit in the dugout, detached from any personal concerns. His lifestyle, his comfort, his thoughts—whether his bed was uncomfortable, how he obtained his food, or if he ever felt bored—were questions we never asked. His moods, his private thoughts about life in the dugout, and even the frequency with which he received letters were matters we left unspoken. He was an enigmatic figure, a man defined solely by his role as an observer.

He was a short and mild-mannered officer, his voice soft, yet there was a certain warmth when the General, who had already taken his leave, paused under the cover of some nearby foliage. The General, with a slight smile and a nod, addressed him by name, "Good-afternoon, Blank," his voice imbued with an unmistakable warmth. It was clear that there was a deeper understanding between them, a mutual appreciation that transcended mere formalities.

"You know—don't you, Blank?—how much I appreciate you." The words were subtle, but they held a depth that was fleeting in the moment. After the brief exchange, as the General began discussing London music halls and the latest performers, the ordinary chatter returned.

On another occasion, I found myself witnessing a rare spectacle—twenty soldiers preparing for a real bombing exercise. The conditions were tense, as they practiced bombing a German trench with live explosives. The young officer in charge, seemingly unfazed by the danger, casually demonstrated how to handle the bombs. "It's perfectly safe," he assured us, "until I take this pin out." With that, he removed the pin, and we observed the men march toward the trench, preparing for the explosion. We were kept at a safe distance, tucked behind whatever cover the terrain offered—nothing more than slight mounds of earth. Sentinels kept watch, ensuring that no one ventured too close. We were instructed to crouch low and protect ourselves. As we huddled behind our makeshift shelter, we heard the thunderous sound of explosions—Bang! Bang! Bang!—accompanied by the high-pitched whine of shrapnel slicing through the air above us. When the smoke finally began to dissipate, we peered over the edge and saw the soldiers rushing forward, braving the bombed-out trench. Miraculously, none of them was injured or killed.

In yet another instance, I had the rare opportunity to witness an entire brigade in action. Several thousand men, accompanied by their transport vehicles, marched in perfect formation, with two Generals observing closely for any sign of imperfection. The display was nothing short of majestic—an awe-inspiring demonstration of military discipline. However, it lacked the rawness I had expected from war. Instead of feeling the tension and chaos of battle, I saw a finely tuned machine. As I watched them march, I began to wonder: if the entire British Army marched by me at this rate, how long would it take for them to pass? I calculated that it would take about three weeks of nonstop observation, without any breaks for meals, to witness the entire force in its entirety. It was an astonishing realization—one that made me even more acutely aware of how elusive the true scale of war remained.

A more vivid image of the military came to me when I visited the baths of a new division—the New Army. There, the soldiers bathed, a momentary respite from the grime of war. The setup was astonishingly British—perhaps more so than the soldiers and officers realized. The baths were housed in a large factory repurposed for this purpose. A young subaltern, no doubt eager to join the fight but consigned to this administrative role, managed the baths. Not only was he the baths keeper, but he also oversaw the laundry operation, ensuring that soldiers could change into clean underwear after their bath. The laundry employed local women and girls, working tirelessly in extremely high temperatures, though none seemed to falter under the heat. After weeks of being surrounded by the harsh, mechanical world of war, the women, with their grace and charm, were a welcome sight. They were stunning—perhaps because they offered a fleeting reminder of the softer, more human side of life, one that had long been absent from our daily existence.

Among the items in the laundry was a peculiar museum display—a collection of shirts that had been worn during the early days of trench warfare, relics of the filth and squalor that had become a part of their wearers. These shirts, according to the experts, were unmatched in their sheer disarray. It was a strange, almost grotesque, tribute to the depths of the war.

The baths themselves were simple, yet efficient—large, steaming vats where soldiers could scrub away the filth of the battlefield. Two hundred and fifty men could bathe, change, and be ready for duty in a single hour. Larger groups could cycle through in a morning, though the true scale of the operation only became clear when I saw entire companies of soldiers marching in, filthy and weary, and emerging freshly cleaned, seemingly more composed and confident. It was a brief moment of respite amid the chaos. The mass of soldiers marching toward the baths, and those marching away, spurred a growing suspicion that a far larger army existed, hidden somewhere in the vicinity.

But despite these glimpses of the military in action, I had yet to truly comprehend the vastness of the Army or its complex infrastructure. I had observed supply lines and streams of resources moving westward, back toward England. There, in the hospitals of Boulogne, I witnessed the next stage of this logistical journey. The process was meticulous, and each step was designed to ensure the soldiers received the best care possible, from the Aid Post to the Advanced Dressing Station, the Field Ambulance, and finally the Casualty Clearing Station. At Boulogne, I saw a hospital where thousands of soldiers received treatment for their wounds. Even at the Clearing Stations, the emphasis was on moving cases quickly—sorting them and sending them onward for further care. Some men, having passed through the initial stages, would eventually board Ambulance Trains or barges, sailing toward England for more intensive treatment.

At Boulogne, the sheer scale of the effort to care for the wounded became apparent. The laundry alone was so vast that it had overtaken the town, with its work sent to England for processing. But even in this environment, the primary objective was to clear the cases—to move them along as quickly as possible to the next stage of care.

One of the most striking sights was the horse hospital. Many of the horses were injured, some with shell wounds, but they were treated with the same care and attention as the men. The sight of a horse undergoing surgery under chloroform left a lasting impression. The animal, having refused to wake after the operation, was gently coaxed back to life. It was impossible to see the horse as anything other than a living, breathing creature, no different from the men who were treated for their wounds.

In the final moments of my time at the front, I caught a glimpse of the true scale of the British Army. I walked along narrow wooden causeways, passing through sandbag walls that formed the frontline defenses. Through a periscope, I saw the enemy positions and the barbed wire that separated us. Men moved in and out of sight, preparing for combat or tending to smaller tasks. The soldiers were ready, but the atmosphere was strangely calm—distant from the chaos of the front lines. As I parted ways with the Major, who had been guiding me through the area, I was struck by the realization of just how different the world I had seen was from the world I had imagined.

"Well, what do you think of our 'trenches'?" the Major asked, his voice tinged with expectation.

"Fine," I responded, though my response was more out of habit than genuine enthusiasm. I wondered if my brief answer had satisfied him.

As I left, I couldn't help but reflect on what I had just witnessed. I understood, for the first time, what war truly was—a complex, relentless machine, grinding away at everything in its path. Yet, I still couldn't shake the feeling that there was so much more beneath the surface, hidden from view. And as I departed, my thoughts turned to the journey ahead, wondering if we would safely navigate the road back.

VI: The Unique City

As we approached Ypres, we encountered a civilian wagon, its contents a mix of furniture from a modest home and several long pieces of gilt picture frame-moulding. The sight of the gleaming gold on the wagon caught our attention amidst the chaos. The wind was unrelenting, strong and warm, whipping up the dust from both the road and the nearby railway track, making the air thick with discomfort. The distant rumble of artillery fire was constant, a reminder of the danger surrounding us. We were urged time and again to hurry past certain areas, to avoid lingering, and the vehicles that carried us were given precise directions on where to take cover during our brief absences.

As we continued, we passed a spot where a shell had struck the ground beside the road, sending a shower of earth and stones crashing onto the roof of an asylum on the opposite side. Strangely, the asylum itself appeared untouched, and the road beneath our feet was unscathed. However, the debris from the blast littered the roof. Despite the signs of destruction around us, we felt little fear; the odds of the picture frame maker escaping with his belongings seemed overwhelmingly in his favor. And indeed, he did. Still, the situation struck a strange chord within me. To an overly sensitive, non-German mind, it seemed almost unjust that the picture-framer, after suffering the loss of his livelihood, should have to risk his life just to salvage the remnants of his once-thriving career.

Further into the city, near its outskirts, we witnessed two men laboring to salvage planks from an upper-floor of a building that had sustained little damage. It was almost all that remained from the structure, and they worked determinedly, risking everything to recover these precious materials. Their efforts, in the context of the broader destruction, seemed almost foolishly heroic.

It had been nearly two decades since I last visited Ypres, and at that time, the city's restoration work had just begun. The restoration of historic landmarks, including the Cloth Hall and the Cathedral of St. Martin, was nearing completion when the war broke out, just in time for the conflict to wreak havoc. This fact, as some Germans argued, reinforced their theory that Belgium, in collusion with Britain, had been preparing for war all along—an absurd yet widely circulated claim. The Grande Place, one of the largest public squares in Europe, was still recognizable. In fact, it was so vast that a medium-sized ocean liner could comfortably fit within it. There were no other squares in London or New York where a 10,000-ton ship could be so easily accommodated. Even a 15,000-ton ship like the Arabic would fit, albeit diagonally.

The Grande Place had witnessed much of history. Back in the 13th century, it had been the heart of a thriving town with a bustling population of 200,000 weavers. Yet, over the centuries, a combination of local mismanagement and foreign aggression had reduced the city's population dramatically. By the 16th century, it was down to 5,000, and by the 20th century, it had shrunk to just over 17,000. Now, it was completely deserted. The city had become uninhabitable. Just months before my visit, the city had been full of life. The people who had fled during the first wave of bombardments began to trickle back in, but their hope was short-lived. By the third week of April, the Grande Place had seen some commerce, with stalls selling postcards depicting the destruction of the railway station. But then came the major bombardment, which, I was told, was still ongoing.

To understand the extent of the devastation, one need only step inside the Cathedral of St. Martin. This Gothic structure, primarily built in the 13th century, had suffered catastrophic damage. The tower, which had remained incomplete since its construction, would never be finished now. Much of the cathedral's body was in ruins. The choir was completely unroofed, and parts of the apse and the Early Gothic nave had been blown apart. The rose window of the south transept, once a breathtaking sight, had been reduced to nothing. Inside, the debris from the destroyed parts of the building piled up like an unrecognizable mountain, covering the once-grand interior. The pile of broken bricks, stones, and dust stretched across 15,000 to 20,000 square feet, rising up to six or seven yards high in places. It was as if the cathedral had been swallowed by the earth itself. Climbing over the mound of rubble was perilous, as it resembled a treacherous mountain range.

Despite the ruin, some remnants of beauty remained. The bright colors of the altar stood in stark contrast to the surrounding devastation, and the organ, miraculously intact, clung to the north wall of the choir. In the sacristy, candelabras and altar furnishings sat yellowed by the corrosive effects of picric acid. From a distance, the cathedral appeared solid, but once inside, the fear that the fragile remains could collapse under the slightest disturbance was palpable.

Leaving the cathedral, I felt a sense of relief, but that feeling was short-lived. Just outside, I was confronted with the destructive force that had caused this devastation. A 17-inch shell had left a crater 50 feet wide, and the explosion had occurred in a graveyard, where the bones of the deceased now lay scattered among the wreckage.

The Cloth Hall, perhaps more impressive than the cathedral itself, had suffered similar, if not worse, damage. The three-story facade, once a marvel of architecture, stood in a state of partial collapse. There was a huge gap on the left side, and the glass was long gone. The facade seemed to lean slightly forward, though I could not tell if it was an optical illusion or an actual shift in its structure. The central tower, though shattered, still held some semblance of its original form. The rest of the building's interior had been reduced to a chaotic mess of rubble. The beautiful Niewwerk, a Renaissance structure at the eastern end of the Cloth Hall, had vanished entirely, along with the nearby Town Hall. Only fragments of arched masonry and piles of debris marked where they once stood.

The area surrounding the Grande Place was no better. Walking around the square, I found myself surrounded by debris and ruin. A few buildings, like the Hopital de Notre Dame, had survived relatively unscathed, though they were still heavily defaced. The rest of the square, however, was little more than a graveyard of shattered walls and crumbled structures. In certain areas, the smell of decay and death lingered in the air, a harsh reminder of the cost of war.

At one point, I paused to make a rough sketch of the scene, hoping to capture the grandeur of the destruction for posterity. The sight before me, with its haunting remnants of once-great buildings, was so striking that I thought the British government had a duty to photograph it properly, to ensure the world saw the scale of the devastation.

I sat on the edge of a shell-hole near the hospital, not daring to get too close for fear the building might collapse. The wind howled around me, and the sound of distant gunfire never stopped. A British plane flew high above, its presence a reminder that the war was far from over. The streets around me were eerily silent, save for the occasional gust of wind or the distant smoke of another burning building. The Grande Place, once a thriving hub of commerce and life, was now a desolate and haunting reminder of the destruction wrought by war.

I whispered to myself, "A shell could land here at any moment."

Fear crept into my heart, but surprisingly, it wasn't the fear of an impending shell that consumed me. No, it was something far more intense: the overwhelming, suffocating loneliness. Cities like Rheims and Arras, though affected by the war, were still inhabited. There were people—postmen, newspapers, shops, even cafes that hummed with the faint rhythm of normal life. But in Ypres, there was nothing. No bustle, no life. Every street felt like an empty desert, devoid of even the most basic signs of existence. Not a single dog scrounged for scraps. The silence was suffocating, heavy like an invisible weight pressing against my chest.

To avoid any confusion, I had made a promise to the Staff officer not to leave my position in the square until he returned. Neither of us wanted to risk wandering through the maze of streets, inadvertently playing a game of hide-and-seek in this grim, deserted town. So, I was left alone, a prisoner to the vast emptiness that surrounded me. I longed desperately for my companions to return.

Suddenly, the sound of voices and footsteps echoed faintly in the distance. Two British soldiers appeared around the corner, slowly walking across the square. Against the vastness of the empty space, they seemed tiny, almost insignificant. I felt a sudden urge to approach them, to speak, but I knew better. Englishmen don't do that, especially in a place like Ypres. We exchanged casual glances—nothing more, nothing less—each of us pretending that everything was perfectly normal.

As long as they were in sight, I felt a strange sense of safety, as if their presence could ward off the growing unease in my chest. But once they disappeared into the distance, the fear returned, stronger than before. It wasn't just fear—it was an all-encompassing sense of dread, an unsettling feeling that gnawed at my nerves and made my mind race with dark thoughts.

I had promised to sketch the scene, so I set to work, but it was more out of obligation than desire. Once the task was done, I sprang to my feet, eager to escape the confines of my little corner. I wandered the streets, hoping to spot my friends returning, but all I found was the same emptiness that had been haunting me. I was depressed, irritable, and honestly regretted my decision to come to the front. I couldn't shake the feeling that I might never leave Ypres alive.

When, at last, I saw the Staff officer approaching, relief flooded through me. But the sense of desolation lingered long after, like a dark cloud that refused to dissipate.

Ypres, like so many places touched by war, had streets that once pulsed with life. One of the main roads, the Rue de Lille, stood out in my memory. It stretched from opposite the Cloth Hall, down to the Lille Gate, and led toward the German lines. This street had been renowned for its stunning architecture. There was the Hospice Belle, a 13th-century shelter for elderly women, the Museum, once the Hotel Merghelynck, full of antiques, and the Hospital of St. John, though not as remarkable as its namesake in Bruges. The Maison de Bois, a beautiful Gothic building, stood proudly at the end of the street, and the Steenen, a fourteenth-century structure, had been converted into the town's post office.

Yet, as I walked down the Rue de Lille now, I was struck by its haunting desolation. Except for the post office, which appeared miraculously intact, the rest of the street lay in ruins. The walls of buildings were reduced to shattered remnants, weeds sprouted from cracks in the stones, and dust swirled in the air, carried by the wind as it swept through the ghostly remnants of the town. The smell of decay was pervasive, rising from the broken masonry that concealed the remnants of the past. It was as if the street itself was mourning the loss of a once-vibrant life.

Turning into a side street, I passed by what seemed to be the homes of lace-makers. These little houses, so humble and inconspicuous, seemed untouched by the devastation. The Germans, with their meticulous precision, would have spared such streets from artillery fire, for they were insignificant in the grand scheme of their destruction. Yet, I couldn't help but wonder how they managed such pinpoint accuracy with their artillery, guided by what must have been incredibly detailed maps. It was rumored that some of these maps had been acquired through deceit, that German agents had posed as citizens to gather intelligence.

Despite the streets seeming untouched, the stillness was unnerving. The doors to the little houses were wide open, revealing rooms in disarray. The small parlors, though disorderly, still contained the remnants of daily life: furniture, once lovingly arranged, now tossed aside in haste. Mantelpieces were cluttered with trinkets, and drawers were left open, not emptied, as though the inhabitants had been abruptly interrupted in their lives.

It was striking how similar these modest homes were to one another, their interiors practically identical in their simplicity. This shared ambition to mirror one another's lives was touching, even in its tragic simplicity. The streets themselves seemed to tell a story of lives interrupted, of women and children hastily fleeing, leaving behind a lifetime of memories and belongings scattered like discarded remnants of their past lives.

Though the interiors were a snapshot of family life—cooking utensils, clothes, small mementos of a life interrupted—I hesitated to venture upstairs. I knew that looting was strictly forbidden, and I respected the rules, though I couldn't help but feel like a visitor in a forgotten world. As I walked from house to house, the eerie stillness overwhelmed me. These homes had once been alive with the rhythm of everyday existence, but now they stood as hollow reminders of what had been lost.

It struck me how quickly everything had changed. A moment ago, these houses had been homes. Then, an alarm—sudden and widespread—swept through the streets, and in the blink of an eye, they became lifeless, abandoned structures, devoid of their former occupants. Where they went, I never asked. It seemed pointless. They had simply vanished, absorbed into the vast sea of refugees.

Beyond the town, the desolate suburbs lay in ruins as well. Factories stood like rusting skeletons, canals were stagnant and forgotten, and railway stations stood silent, abandoned to the encroaching weeds. It felt as though time itself had stopped, leaving only the wreckage of what had once been a thriving community.

Not far beyond the outskirts, the German artillery positions lay, their guns aimed directly at the heart of Ypres. These were the weapons of destruction, guided by men who had devoted their lives to perfecting the art of annihilation. Around them were soldiers, once free men, now reduced to mere instruments of war, carrying out orders with brutal efficiency.

Each shell that rained down on Ypres was a product of meticulous planning, a direct result of orders that had been weighed and decided with careful calculation. The destruction of this ancient town was not random; it was a purposeful, deliberate effort to erase something beautiful. The generals, their faces filled with grim satisfaction, would celebrate each successful hit. "Another shell in the Cathedral!" they would exclaim. "A hole in the Cloth Hall!" And so, Ypres was slowly reduced to rubble, its centuries-old history shattered.

"But," you might say, "this is war, after all." And yes, perhaps that is true. But even in war, there are moments when we pause to reflect on the tragedy of it all.

The future of Ypres, though uncertain, remains a subject that captivates the imagination. While it is but one of many cities that have endured terrible suffering, it undoubtedly holds a unique place in history. Many smaller towns and villages have experienced destruction similar to Ypres, and in some cases, they may have even endured more devastation. However, no city with the same level of historical, commercial, and artistic significance has suffered to the same extent as Ypres has so far. It stands as a tragic symbol of the devastation wrought by German forces in Belgium during the war.

Ypres sat on the road to Calais, but its proximity to this strategic path was not the real cause of its destruction. Even if the German guns had not reduced the city to ruins, the path to Calais would not have become any easier for their military machine. Ypres was never intended to be a military stronghold, and it could not have served as one. Had the Germans been able to defeat the British forces stationed near Ypres, they would have been able to pass through the city with little resistance, like a predator through an unprotected field.

The real crime of Ypres was its unfortunate location. It lay in the path of a frustrated and enraged enemy army, one that, despite its overwhelming numerical superiority and immense firepower, could not shift the small but determined British force in the area. The German forces, brimming with arrogance and overconfidence, were understandably furious at their inability to break through. In their fury, they sought to destroy something—anything—to relieve their frustration. The result was the destruction of Ypres' most treasured architectural and cultural landmarks, such as the Cathedral and Cloth Hall, which crumbled under the weight of their misplaced rage. The city's trenches, however, remained intact.

This destruction of Ypres, while senseless, carries a certain psychological truth. It was the result of an overwhelming sense of impotence, a desperate need to destroy something when victory could not be achieved on the battlefield. This psychological reality provides insight into why Ypres, the city of history and beauty, was reduced to rubble. It marks the end of a chapter in the city's history and the beginning of a new, uncertain future.

To understand the future of Ypres, it is essential to assess the damage it has sustained. Although the city has been devastated, it is not completely destroyed. When I visited in July, I found that about half of the buildings in Ypres were still standing, albeit in a damaged state. While these structures are marred by the ravages of war, many can be swiftly repaired. The residents of Ypres, many of whom were displaced, could return to their homes with minimal difficulty, provided the economic conditions are favorable. It is inevitable that the economic situation will improve, as Belgium's industrious people will rebuild what has been lost.

However, the city's most iconic structures—the ones that stood at the heart of Ypres' civic and cultural life—are gone. Take the Grande Place, for example, which has been utterly destroyed. If Ypres is to recover in any way resembling its former glory, the buildings that once lined the Grande Place will need to be completely rebuilt. This will require an immense effort, as the foundations of these structures are buried beneath the rubble. I estimate that there were at least 150 privately owned buildings on the Grande Place, each with multiple stories, and each one was once a vital source of income and livelihood for the people who owned them. Those who once called Ypres home are now scattered across Europe, impoverished and disheartened. The same devastation extends to other significant streets like the Rue de Lille.

If the owners of Ypres' properties were to return and attempt to rebuild, the scale of the task would be overwhelming. It would demand immense initiative, resilience, and a faith in the future that could daunt even the most audacious among them. Furthermore, the task of rebuilding will be hindered by a lack of both financial capital and labor, as Europe is in the throes of recovery from the war. The labor shortage will likely be more acute than the financial one, as every sector will require workers. The immense scale of reconstruction, from clearing the foundations to refurnishing homes and finding tenants, will make this a daunting, perhaps impossible, task.

In a way, Ypres will never fully recover. The city, if rebuilt, will be a shadow of its former self, a reminder of the horrors that once took place there. The new Ypres will be a camp amidst the ruins, a temporary settlement where people gather but never fully return to the city's former vitality. For generations to come, if not forever, Ypres will remain a testament to the senseless violence of war and the folly of those who caused it.

In the immediate aftermath of the war, Ypres is likely to become a place of historical significance. It will attract tourists and sightseers from all corners of the world. Hotels and guides will spring up, and tourists will visit the ruins in droves, eager to witness the destruction firsthand. Some people will undoubtedly profit from this macabre spectacle, turning the city's tragedy into a source of income. This is a grim fate for the people of Ypres, but it is an inevitable one. The greater the number of people who visit Ypres and learn of its history, the greater the hope for humanity's progress.

If the Cloth Hall's façade can be preserved, it should bear an inscription commemorating the events of July 31, 1914, when Germany assured Belgium that it would respect its neutrality, only to violate that promise just days later. The inscription would read:

"On July 31st, 1914, The German Minister At Brussels Gave A Positive And Solemn Assurance That Germany Had No Intention Of Violating The Neutrality Of Belgium. Four Days Later The German Army Invaded Belgium. Look Around."

As you walk through the ruins of Ypres, one cannot help but feel a mixture of contempt and anger at the German government's shameless attempts to justify its actions. The excuses offered by Germany for its actions—mean, misguided, and absurd—stand in stark contrast to the reality of the city's destruction. Yet, there is a certain grim satisfaction in knowing that Germany will one day regret the crime it has committed. The leaders who once boasted of their military prowess now face the consequences of their actions and are likely shaking in their boots as they prepare to face the inevitable fallout from their hubris and barbarism.

THE END